Table of Contents

ÇA ROULE?

What's French IRL?

Bonjour! I'm a French language pro from Paris, living in London, with over 15 years of teaching under my beret. And let me tell you, textbooks aren't enough to conquer the French language. You need to get how the locals really speak!

That's where French IRL comes in handy, revealing the most commonly used slang expressions. We're not talking stiff book talk here. We're talking real-life French! With us, you'll be able to chat like a true local!

Our approach is anything but boring. Prepare to have a blast while you master those tricky French phrases.

On y va!

Illustrations by Aimee Irving.

Special thanks to Bobby Kane.

Raphaël Mura

1.Jean From The Arrondissement.

EMBRACE YOUR INNER PARISIAN: TIPS FOR BLENDING IN WHILE VISITING THE CITY OF LIGHT:

Imagine you're meeting up with a friend in Paris, but you're feeling like an obvious tourist. That's the last thing you want! Instead, take a cue from Jenny From The Block and channel "Jean From The Arrondissement". Use local slang to blend in with the Parisians!

"APÉRO"
.pe.ʁo/
glish: pre-dinner drink.
onunciation: "ah-peh-roh".

"TRANQUILLE"
/tʁɑ̃.kil/
English: I'm chill.
Literal: easygoing.
Pronunciation:
"trahng-keel".

ROULE?"
ʁul/
glish: how's it going?
eral: what's rolling?
onunciation: "sa rool".

"JE KIFFE GRAVE"
/ʒə kif gʁav/
English: I dig this.
Derived from the Arabic word "kif" which means well-being, pleasure.
Pronunciation: "kif"

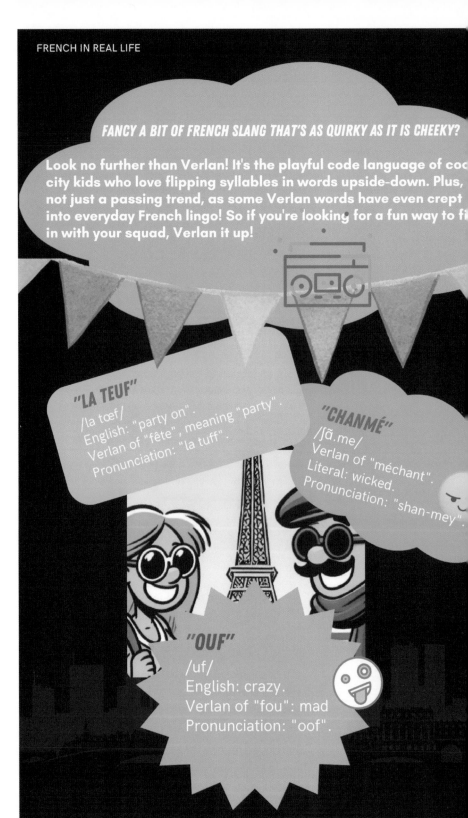

FANCY A BIT OF FRENCH SLANG THAT'S AS QUIRKY AS IT IS CHEEKY?

Look no further than Verlan! It's the playful code language of coo
city kids who love flipping syllables in words upside-down. Plus,
not just a passing trend, as some Verlan words have even crept
into everyday French lingo! So if you're looking for a fun way to fi
in with your squad, Verlan it up!

"LA TEUF"
/la tœf/
English: "party on".
Verlan of "fête", meaning "party".
Pronunciation: "la tuff".

"CHANMÉ"
/ʃã.me/
Verlan of "méchant".
Literal: wicked.
Pronunciation: "shan-mey".

"OUF"
/uf/
English: crazy.
Verlan of "fou": mad
Pronunciation: "oof".

2. Garçon! : Ordering at the table.

SURVIVING FRENCH WAITERS:

We've all been there: you walk into a café in Paris and suddenly the server treats you like you just called him a "Petit Filou!" . Pas de problème ; you can use these handy phrases to impress them and show that you're a confident customer. Speak like a local and earn their respect!
Oh, and the French never use "Garçon!" in a bistrot to call the waiter. It's outdated and rude...

NO ONE WANTS TO BE MR BEAN IN THAT LOBSTER RESTAURANT!

CHECK OUT A DIALOGUE BETWEEN HIP NATURAL WINE AFICIONADOS AND A (MOODY) PARISIAN BARTENDER:

Client: Salut, salut! C'est sympa par ici, vous vendez du vin nature?
Customer: Hey, hey! It's nice around here. Do you guys sell natural wine?

Serveur: Ouais, c'est possible. Vous êtes du coin?
Waiter: Yeah, maybe. Are you locals?

Client: Non, on est anglais, mais on traîne à Bastille depuis cet été.
Customer: Nah, we're English, but we've been hanging out in Bastille since this summer.

Serveur: Anglais, hein... et vous pensez vous y connaître en vin... haha.
Waiter: English, huh... and you think you know your wine... haha.

Client: Ah ça, pas de problème. Ça fait 10 piges que j'en bois! J'suis à fond dedans. Vous avez un menu?
Customer: Oh, no problem. I've been drinking natural wines for 10 years. I'm really into it. Can I see the menu?

Serveur: Bon, si vous le dites.
Waiter: Well, if you say so.

Client: Franchement, c'est pas l'habit qui fait le moine, vous savez.
Customer: Honestly, you can't judge a book by its cover, you know.

Serveur: OK, voilà la carte des vins. Vous voulez manger un truc? On peut vous sortir un plateau fromage-charcuterie ou un croque-monsieur tout simple.
Waiter: OK, here's the wine list. Do you want something to eat? We can bring out a cheese and charcuterie platter or a simple croque-monsieur.

Client: Ah ouais, ça a l'air top, mais en fait, je suis végétarien.
Customer: Oh yeah, that sounds awesome, but I'm actually a vegetarian.

Serveur: En France, les végétariens, ça n'existe pas!
Waiter: In France, vegetarians don't exist!

Client: Ah ben si, vous savez, c'est de plus en plus à la mode. Vous pourriez me faire un croque monsieur sans le jambon?
Customer: Oh yes, you know, it's becoming more and more trendy. Could you make me a croque monsieur without the ham?

Serveur: Sans jambon? Mais vous êtes pas un peu perché, vous? Ça c'est plus un croque monsieur, c'est même pas un croque rien du tout, d'ailleurs...
Waiter: Without ham? Are you a bit out there? That's not really a croque monsieur; it's not even a croque anything, for that matter...

Client: Bah si, c'est un Croque-Mademoiselle, avec des légumes. Et sans jambon pour l'occasion.
Customer: Well, yes, it's a croque mademoiselle, with vegetables. And without ham for the occasion.

Serveur: Un croque mademoiselle. Vous êtes un petit rigolo, vous! Bon, allez, c'est parti.
Waiter: A croque mademoiselle. You're a little joker, you! Alright, let's do it.

Some key expressions:

"ÊTRE DU COIN"
/ɛtʁə dy kwɛ̃/
English: to be local.
Literal: to be from the corner.
Pronunciation: "et-ruh doo kwah"

"TRAÎNER"
/tʁɛ.ne/
English: to hang out.
Literal: to drag, to pull, to linger.
Pronunciation: ""treh-ney".

"UNE PIGE"
/yn pjɛʒ/
English: a year (slang).
Literal: a stint.
Pronunciation in French: "ewn peezh".

BE THE COOLEST CAT IN PARIS

c'est
gétarien!

PARIS

"L'HABIT NE FAIT PAS LE MOINE"
/l.abi nə fɛ pa lə mwan/
English: don't judge a book by its cover.
Literal: "The clothes don't make the monk".
One's appearance does not reflect one's true character.
Pronunciation in French: "lah-bee nuh feh pah luh mwan".

"C'EST TOP"
/se tɔp/
English: it's top-notch.
Pronunciation: "say top".

"ÊTRE PERCHÉ"
/ɛtʁə peʃe/
English: in an unconventional or eccentric state.
Literal: to be perched or elevated physically.
Pronunciation: "et-ruh pesh-ey".

"RIGOLO"
/ri.go.lo/
English: funny or amusing.
Pronunciation: "ree-goh-loh".

3. Dating like a local.

FRANCE, THE ENCHANTING COUNTRY OF ROMANCE!

But hey, if your approach is more vintage robot than smooth operator from the roaring twenties, it might be time to dial down the automaton vibes. Loosen up a bit! Channel your inner Jacques Dutronc or Françoise Hardy . Be like James Bond minus the old-ham or "vieux jambon". Time to sparkle, not creak! Here are a few expressions to up your dating game:

DRAGUER
/dra-ge/
English: to flirt.
Pronunciation: "dra-geh" .

F RENCARDER
ə rɑ̃.kaʀ.de/
nglish: to make plans for a date.
onunciation: "suh rahn-kar-dey".

UN COUP DE FOUDRE
/œ̃ ku də fu.dʀə/
English: love at first sight.
Literal: a lightning strike.
Pronunciation: "uhn koo duh
oo-druh".

CHATTING TO A FRIEND ABOUT YOUR DATE:

Alors ton date?

On va se rencarder 2m1!

T'as matché hier! Coup de foudre?

Je l'ai trop dragué direct!

Il est sympa?

Grave!

Tu vas choper!

Première date depuis que j'ai largué mon ex!

J'croise les doigts pour toi! A+

FRENCH IN REAL LIFE

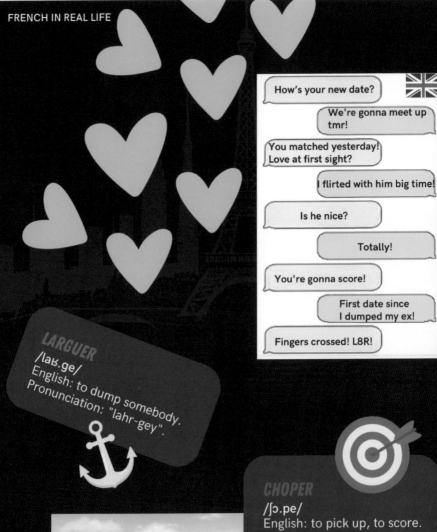

How's your new date?

We're gonna meet up tmr!

You matched yesterday! Love at first sight?

I flirted with him big time!

Is he nice?

Totally!

You're gonna score!

First date since I dumped my ex!

Fingers crossed! L8R!

LARGUER
/laʁ.ge/
English: to dump somebody.
Pronunciation: "lahr-gey".

CHOPER
/ʃɔ.pe/
English: to pick up, to score.
Pronunciation: "sho-pey".

4. Texting & social media

THE FRENCH SURE KNOW HOW TO TECH!

Imagine this: you're texting your French buddies, and suddenly they throw a "mdr" at you. What does it mean? Well, it's not some mysterious acronym; it's just the French way of saying "lol" ("mort de rire = "dead of laughter"), so laughing out loud in their own stylish way. Let's explore some more:

"T"
bbreviation for "salut": hi.
onunciation: "sah-loo"

"CC"
Abbreviation for "coucou" often used to greet someone casually.
Pronunciation: " "coo-coo".

"STP"
bbreviation for "s'il te plaît,"
s in please.
onunciation: "seel tuh pleh"

"K"
bbreviation for
pourquoi": why
Pronunciation:"poor-kwah".

"MERCI BCP"
Abbreviation for "merci beaucoup": thank you very much.
Pronunciation: "mare-see boh-koo".

"TKT"
Abbreviation for "t'inquiète": don't worry.
Pronunciation: "tan-kee-yet".

"ATT"
Abbreviation for "attends": wait.
Pronunciation: "ah-tahn".

"JTM"
Abbreviation for "je t'aime": I love you.
Pronunciation: "zhuh tem".

11

"CPG"
Abbreviation for "c'est pas grave" : no big deal.
Pronunciation: "say pah grav".

"ECT"
Abbreviation for "éco...
listen.
Pronunciation: "ay-kc...

"DR"
Abbreviation for "de rien": you're welcome.
Pronunciation: "duh ryan".

"2M1"
Abbreviation for "dema...
tomorrow.
Similar to "2moro".
Pronunciation: "duh-m...

SOCIAL MEDIA KEY WORDS AND EXPRESSIONS:

"SE CONNECTER"
/sə kɔ.nɛk.te/
English: To log in.
Pronunciation: "suh koh-nek-tey".

"SUIVRE"
1.7K
/sɥivʁ/
English: To follow.
Pronunciation: "sweev".

"S'ABONNER"
/sa.bɔ.ne/
English: To subscribe.
Pronunciation: "sa-bohn-ey".

"UN COMMENTAIRE"
/œ̃. kɔ.mɑ̃.tɛʁ/
English: A comment.
Pronunciation: "uhn koh-r...

5. Le shopping

...HING YOUR INNER FASHIONISTA WITH A TRIP TO FRANCE?

...aute couture to street style, France has been dominating the ...scene for years. Don't sweat about packing your grandma's ...socks, as you'll find everything you need to channel that ...French fashion. To shop like a boss and ooze that French je ...quoi, you just need to brush up on a few buzzwords in the ...We've got you covered!

HERE'S A DIALOGUE BETWEEN A CUSTOMER
AND THE VENDOR IN A VINTAGE CLOTHING SHOP:

Client: Sympa votre friperie! **Je cherche un pull stylé, genre décontracté?**
Customer: Nice vintage shop!. I'm looking for a stylish, kind of casual sweater?

Vendeur: Absolument, je comprends. On a quelques vêtements d'occasion **qui pourraient vous plaire. Venez, je vous montre.**
Salesperson: Absolutely, I get it. We have a few second-hand clothes that you might like. Come, let me show you.

Client: Nickel, **merci ! Oh, au fait, y'a des promos en ce moment ou c'est le prix normal ?** Customer: Sweet, thanks! Oh, by the way, are there any promotions going on right now, or is it the regular price?

Vendeur: En ce moment, on a une promo : deux pulls pour le prix d'un. Plutôt cool, non ?
Salesperson : Right now, we have a promotion: two sweaters for the price of one. Pretty cool, huh?

Client: Ah, carrément ! Pas reuch! **Et** niveau taille, **c'est standard ici ?**
Customer: Oh, definitely! Cheap! And size-wise, is it standard here?

Vendeur: Ouais, on a une coupe assez standard. Mais si vous voulez un truc un peu plus ajusté, je peux vous montrer les tailles disponibles.
Salesperson: Yeah, we have a fairly standard fit. But if you want something a bit more fitted, I can show you the available sizes.

Client: Parfait. J'aime bien fouiner un peu. Et, euh, les cabines d'essayage, **c'est où ? Customer:**
Perfect. I like to browse a bit. And, um, where are the fitting rooms?

Vendeur: Juste là-bas, à droite. Si vous avez besoin d'une autre taille ou de quelque chose, faites-moi signe.
Salesperson: Right over there, to the right. If you need another size or anything, just give me a shout.

Client: Merci ! Cool, je vais essayer ça. Ah, au fait, on paie par carte bleue **ou** en liquide **ici ?**
Customer: Thanks! Cool, I'll try these on. Oh, and, Is it cash or card here?

Vendeur : Vous pouvez régler **par carte ou** en espèces**, Pas de souci.**
Salesperson: Yep, you can pay by card or cash. No problem.

Client : Super, je paie en liquide, j'ai pas assez de thune **sur ma carte.**
Customer: Great, I'll pay cash, I don't have enough dough on my card.

Some key expressions:

"UNE FRIPERIE"
/fʁipʁi/
English: thrift or vintage shop.
Pronunciation: "free-puh-ree".

"D'OCCASION"
/dɔ.ka.zjɔ̃/
English: Second-hand.
Pronunciation: "doh-ka-zhyon".

"NICKEL"
/nikəl/
English: Awesome.
Pronunciation: "nee-kel".

"PAS REUCH"
/pah reuhsh/
English: Not expensive.
Verlan of: "cher": expensive.
Pronunciation: "pah reuhsh".

"NIVEAU TAILLE"
/niv-o tai/
English: in terms of size.
Literal: le niveau: the level.
la taille: the size.
Pronunciation: "nee-voh tahy".

"EN ESPÈCES"
/ɑ̃ ɛs.pɛs/
English: In cash
Pronunciation: "ahn ess-pess".

"LA CABINE D'ESSAYAGE"
/ka.bin dɛ.sɛ.jaʒ/
English: Fitting room.
Pronunciation: "kah-been deh-say-ahzh".

"FAITES-MOI SIGNE"
/fɛt mwa siɲ/
English: Let me know.
Literal: "Give me a sign".
Pronunciation: "fet mwah seen".

"LA CARTE BLEUE"
/kaʁt blø/
English: Credit card.
Pronunciation: "kart bluh".

"EN LIQUIDE"
/ɑ̃ li.kid/
English: In cash
Literal: In liquid
Pronunciation: "ahn lee-keed".

"RÉGLER"
/ʁe.ʒle/
English: To pay or settle
Pronunciation: "ray-gley".

"LA THUNE"
/tyn/
English: Dough (money)
Pronunciation: "tune".

6. À la plage

GET READY TO SIZZLE LIKE A LOCAL UNDER THE CÔTE D'AZUR SUN!

Summer's here, and you're ready to paint the town red in the chicest way possible. But don't think you can just breeze in and blend in! No worries, though... Take a chill pill and be the star of your own French 60's flick, just like the stylish folks in those iconic Eric Rohmer films.

"SE POSER"
/sə poz-e/
English: To chill or to relax.
Pronunciation: "suh poz-ey".

"FAIRE TREMPETTE"
/fɛʀ tʀɑ̃.pɛt/
English: To take a dip
Literal: To soak.
Pronunciation: "fehr trahmp-peht".

"BOUQUINER"
/bukine/
English: To read a book leisurely, especially at the beach.
Pronunciation: "boo-keen-ey".

"BOIRE UN VERRE"
/bwaʀ œ̃ vɛʀ/
English: To have a drink.
Literal: "To drink a glass".
Pronunciation: "bwah-ruh uh(n) vair".

"AVOIR LA FLEMME"
/a.vwaʀ la flɛm/
English: To feel lazy.
Pronunciation: "ah-vwahr lah flem".

"SE DORER LA PILULE"
/sə do.ʀe la pi.lyl/
English: To sunbathe.
Literal: To gild the pill.
Pronunciation: "suh doh-reh lah pee-lool".

"DORMIR À LA BELLE ÉTOILE"
/dɔʀ.miʀ a la bɛl e.twal/
English: To sleep under the stars.
Pronunciation: "dor-meer ah lah bel eh-twahl".

"FAIRE LA BRINGUE"
/fɛʀ la bʀɛ̃g/
English: To party. "Faire la fête".
Pronunciation: "fehr lah brang".

More key words:

"BRONZER"
/brɔ̃.ze/
English: To tan or to sunbathe.
Pronunciation: "bronz-ey".

"LA RANDONNÉE PALMÉE"
/rɑ̃.dɔ.ne pal.me/
English: Snorkeling.
Pronunciation: "rahn-doh-nay palm-ay".

"LES LUNETTES DE SOLEIL"
/ly.nɛt də sɔ.lɛj/
English: Sunglasses.
Pronunciation: "loo-net deh soh-ay".

"LA CANICULE"
/ka.ni.kyl/
English: Heatwave.
Pronunciation: "ka-nee-kool".

"BOIRE LA TASSE"
/bwaʁ la tas/
English: Involuntarily swallowing water when swimming.
Literal: "Drink the cup".
Pronunciation: "bwahr lah tahs".

"UN COUP DE SOLEIL"
/ku də sɔ.lɛj/
English: A sunburn.
Literal: A hit of sun.
Pronunciation: "koo duh soh-lei".

HERE'S A MOTHER-DAUGHTER CHAT À LA PLAGE TO ILLUSTRATE:

Mère: Salut ma chérie, comment ça s'est passé la journée à la plage?
Mother: Hi sweetheart, how was your day at the beach?

Fille: Trop bien, maman! On a fait trempette, **on s'est** doré la pilule, **mais j'ai pris un un** coup de soleil. La canicule a **mis tout le monde à plat, mais on a quand même** fait la bringue!
Daughter: It was awesome, Mum! We took a dip, soaked up the sun, but I got a sunburn. The heatwave hit us hard, but we still had a blast partying!

Mère: Vous avez fait quoi d'autre?
Mère: What else did you do?

Fille: On a pris l'apéro, **j'ai tenté de** bouquiner, **mais finalement, j'ai eu** la flemme. **Et devine quoi? J'ai failli** boire la tasse **en faisant de** la randonnée palmée!
Daughter: We had an aperitif, I tried to read a bit but ended up feeling lazy. Oh, and guess what? Almost swallowed some seawater while snorkeling!

7. Nightlife.

YOU'VE GOTTA FIGHT. FOR YOUR RIGHTS. TO PARTY!

FUN!

So you're ready to be the dancing queen/king at the Rex Club in Paris but you're
feeling a little perplexed when it comes to ordering drinks or engaging the conversation with the coolest kids in the discothèque? No problem, we got you covered! Check out these expressions and boogie with extra oulala!

"GUEULE DE BOIS"
/gœl də bwa/ English: Hangover.
Literal: "Wooden mouth or face".
Pronunciation: "gul du bwah".

ENDRE LA POIRE"
dʁ la pwaʁ/ English: To
one's sides laughing.
ral: "to split the pear".
onunciation: "suh fahndruh lah
var".

BOURRÉ"
ʁe/
n: To be drunk.
To be full.
nciation: "et-ruh boo-rey".

E LÂCHER"
sə laʃ-e/
nglish: To let loose or to go wild.
iteral: To let oneself go.
Pronunciation: "suh lah-shey".

"SE DÉHANCHER"
/sə de.ã.ʃ-e/ English: To sway or groove/ English: To sway or groove (with hip mouvement).
Pronunciation: "suh deh-ahnsh-ey".

"LA CHOUILLE"
/ʃuj/
nglish: A party or a lively
athering.
onunciation: "shwee".

"S'ÉCLATER"
/se e.kla.te/
English: To have a lot of fun.
Literal: To burst or explode.
Pronunciation: "sey-klah-tey".

19

HERE'S A PHONE CONVO BETWEEN 2 FRIENDS GETTING READY TO HIT THE CLUB!

Ami 1: Yo, ça roule?
Friend 1: Yo, what's up?

Ami 2: Tranquille, tranquille. Ça te dit de bouger en boîte ce soir?
Friend 2: Chillin', chillin'. You up for hitting the club tonight?

Ami 1: Grave! On commence par un verre? Un petit "Gin To" avant?
Friend 1: Totally! How about starting with a drink? A little "G & T" before?

Ami 2: Carrément, on se fait un happy hour! On se fait une chouille avant!
Friend 2: For sure, let's do happy hour! Let's have a little pre-party!

Ami 1: Y'a un DJ mortel au Rex. Y'a moyen de se déhancher un peu.
Friend 1: There's a killer DJ at Rex. We can sway a little.

Ami 2: On va bien kiffer!
Friend 2: We're gonna have a blast!

Ami 1: Grave, on peut bien délirer. Je vais essayer de pas être trop bourré, j'ai trop de taff lundi.
Friend 1: Totally, should be trippy. I'll try not to get too drunk, I have too much work to do on Monday.

Ami 2: Parfait, mec! Bois de l'eau avant pour pas être gueule de bois demain! Alors, on se capte là-bas?
Friend 2: Perfect, mate! Drink lots of water so you don't get hungover tomorrow! So, catch you there.

Ami 1: Ouais, je me prépare!
Friend 1: Yeah, getting ready!

More key words:

"MORTEL"
/mɔʁ.tɛl/
English: killer, awesome.
Literal: deadly.
Pronunciation: "mor-tel".

EN BOÎTE"
...ɔ̃.ze/
...nglish: At the club.
...ronunciation: "ã bwat".

"KIFFER"
/ki.fe/
English: To love, to dig.
Pronunciation: "kee-fey".

"Y'A MOYEN"
/ja mwajɛ̃/
English: It's possible.
Pronunciation: "yah mwah-yen".

"LE TAFF"
/taf/
English: Job or work.
Slang for: Travail.
Pronunciation: "taf".

"ON SE CAPTE"
/ɔ̃ sə kapt/
English: Catch you later.
Pronunciation: "on suh capt".

7. Culture.

The French like their culture!

You're now practically a real local French person: clicking your fingers out about town, a master of shopping, a beach boss, a club OG... But wait a minute! There's nothing worse than being a snooty tourist when it comes to navigating cinemas, theatres, museums and galleries. Be like The Fresh Prince of Ballard-Créteil and use these awesome local words!

"LE CINOCHE"
/sinɔʃ/
English: The cinema, the movies.
Pronunciation: "see-nosh".

"ÇA DÉCHIRE"
/sa de.ʃiʁ/
English: it's awesome.
Literal: "It rips".
Pronunciation: "sah deh-sheer".

"UNE EXPO"
/ɛkspo/
English: exhibition.
Pronunciation: "ehk-spo".

"UN NAVET"
/navɛ/
English: A flop, bad movie or performance.
Literal: A turnip.
Pronunciation: "nah-vey".

"UN CARTON"
/kaʁ.tɔ̃/
English: A hit (movie).
Literal: A cardboard.
Pronunciation: "kar-tohn".

"BRANCHÉ"
/bʁɑ̃.ʃe/
English: Trendy.
Literal: Plugged in
Pronunciation: "brahn-shaey"

"CRÈME DE LA CRÈME"
/kʀɛm də la kʀɛm/
English: The cream of the crop.
Pronunciation: "krem duh lah krem".

TER UN COUP D'ŒIL"
te œ ku dœj/
ish: To take a quick look.
al: "To throw a glance".
unciation: "zhuh-teuh uhn
duh œy".

(E) MORDU(E)"
ʀ.dy/
ish: Passionate about a specific
ity.
al: bitten.
nunciation: "mor-doo".

"AVOIR UN COUP DE CŒUR"
/avwaʀ œ̃ ku də kœʀ/
English: To have deep admiration for
a piece of art or an artist.
Pronunciation: "av-wahr uhn
koo duh kur".

"EN METTRE PLEIN LA VUE"
/ã mɛtʀ plɛ̃ la vy/
English: To impress or dazzle.
Literal: "To put a lot in the eyes."
Pronunciation: "ahn met treh plehn
lah vew".

"CHINER"
/ʃi.ne/
English: browse through antiques
or secondhand items.
Pronunciation: "shee-ney".

Amie 1: Salut Sophie! Ça va bien ?
Friend 1: Hi! How are you doing?

Amie 2: Salut Marine ! Ouais, tranquille. J'étais au cinoche **hier soir, puis je suis allée à une** expo **d'art contemporain ce matin.**
Friend 2: Hey Marine! Yeah, good. I went to the cinema last night, then I visited a contemporary art exhibition this morning.

Amie 1: Oh, sympa ! Tu as vu quelque chose de cool ?
Friend 1: Oh, nice! Did you see something cool?

Amie 2: Ouais, il y a une expo de Magritte qui déchire **bien à Pompidou. Par contre, le film, je te raconte pas...**
Friend 2: Yeah, there's a Magritte exhibition at Pompidou that's really awesome. But the movie, I won't even tell you...

Amie 1: Ah mince, vraiment ? Qu'est-ce que c'était ?
Friend 1: Oh no, really? What was it?

Amie 2: Un film soi-disant branché**, mais c'était un vrai** navet**. Ça fait genre un** carton **en ce moment apparement. Les effets spéciaux en** mettent plein la vue **mais le scénario est bidon.**
Friend 2: A supposedly trendy film, but it was a real dud. It's supposedly a hit right now. The special effects are impressive, and the storyline is rubbish.

Amie 1: Dommage. Justement, je pensais bouger dans un musée cet aprèm. Ça te dit d'aller jeter un coup d'œil **?**
Friend 1: Too bad. I was actually thinking of checking out a museum this afternoon. How about going to take a look?

Amie 2: Carrément ! On pourrait chiner **un peu dans les galeries du quartier.**
Friend 2: Absolutely! We could also explore some galleries in the neighbourhood.

Amie 1: Excellente idée! Je suis assez mordue **d'art moderne en ce moment mais on peut voir autre chose.**
Friend 1: Excellent idea! I'm quite into modern art at the moment, but we can check out something else.

Amie 2: Palais de Tokyo, ça te chauffe?
Friend 2: How about Palais de Tokyo?

Amie 1: Parfait, ça roule. À tout à l'heure !
Friend 1: Perfect, sounds good. See you in a bit!

Printed in Poland
by Amazon Fulfillment
Poland Sp. z o.o., Wrocław

31119869R00016